E M

Grace

HELPING YOU NAVIGATE THROUGH
YOUR PAIN AND SUFFERING

Joy M. Briscoe

Exhibiting God's grace as a believer is important; however, this can be a challenge without first embracing His grace for yourself. Navigating through life's challenges, circumstances and setbacks sometimes make it difficult to receive the fullness of love God has for us.

In the book, *Embrace Grace*, Joy transparently shares her life's journey, including battling illness and family conflict, in such a relatable way that the reader is compelled to experience God's grace for themselves, regardless of how "messy" they perceive their own lives to be.

This book masterfully teaches the importance of applying God's word to the hardships presented in life. It is both timely and necessary in our current environment.

—First Lady Trina Jenkins,
First Baptist Church of Glenarden

I have had the honor of representing many influential clients. When I ask them, what is their "why", I look for a story that moves me on every level. Mentally, emotionally, physically, and spiritually. Author Joy M. Briscoe has done just that. Hearing her story ignited me to not only share her purpose, but help her translate this inspirational content into a multitude of opportunities.

Author Briscoe illustrates in her book that we are placed here on this earth to pour into broken spaces by sharing the vulnerable stories of our lives in order to help elevate people to new levels, frequencies and spiritual heights. We all grow from experience, and have gone through many obstacles in life. Author Briscoe shows through example this journey is not asking us to play the victim nor think we are superior to others when we've made it to the other side; however, understand the act of gratitude in the midst of the storm and see God's grace despite it all.

Embrace Grace is a literary description of God's merciful love. This book is a testament and reminder that what God has for you no matter what the circumstances look like today...is for you and only you! Author Joy Briscoe inspires me continuously and reminds me of the goodness of the kingdom through her life's story. As her publicist, her dear friend and sister in Christ it is with great honor that I highly recommend this book to each person looking for comfort, rest and a gentle reminder that the Lord God is our restoration, provider and sustainer in all things mind, body, soul, and spirit.

-Porsha Green PR
CEO, Purpose PR Agency, LLC

Dedication

This book is dedicated to the ones who became my full-time care-takers in the season I couldn't take care of myself, my husband and children—Rev. Vincent, Vincent Eric, Janae, Janelle, and Elijah Briscoe.

Acknowledgments

Husband: Words cannot express just how grateful I am. I wish my human nature of not always having the perfect response wouldn't get in the way of me demonstrating consistently just how thankful I am for you. Thank you for sacrificing your power and position and, through your humility, serving and taking care of me. Thank you for staying faithfully by my side and suffering with me. Thank you for helping me to relearn how to walk confidently, not just in the physical but in the spiritual, as well as how to take care of myself all over again. You truly have turned one of our greatest tragedies into one of our greatest love stories.

Children, to each of you: Vincent Eric, Janae, Janelle, and Elijah. Thank you for taking on my responsibilities at such a young age to assist Dad in becoming my caretaker. Thank you for every time you told a friend you couldn't play or come to their events because you had to babysit your mom. Thank you for your compassion and patience to love me and wait for me to get better.

Parents: Pastor Matthew and Minister Darlene Gallashaw have always been known as Dad and Mom to me. Thank you for your love, prayers, and being two of my biggest supporters. You have always believed in the God in me and seen what He was doing in my life, even in the midst of the greatest disasters in my life.

Pastor John K. Jenkins Sr. and *First Lady Trina Jenkins:* Thank you for modeling before me what grace looks like. You've shown me grace is not about what all I can get; grace operates through the strength in all I can give through my heartfelt love, patience, honesty, integrity, and mercy. Thank you for providing for me through our church The First Baptist Church of Glenarden, the greatest, firmest foundation that helped me stand in the midst of life's roughest storms.

Rev. Frederick C. Johnson, also known as my *spiritual doctor*: Thank you for praying and fasting for me, as well as for not letting go until God answered you on my behalf. He gave you a word and instructions for me. You truly didn't let time or distance remove your love and care for me.

Pastor Joy Morgan, my spiritual twin and birthing coach: Thank you for helping me give birth to this book. Your continual support has been encouragement and fuel for me through this process! For every call, every workshop, every prayer, every text, and every DM, thank you!

Two of my best friends, First Ladies Kim Henderson and *Terrie Stevenson*: Words cannot express just how much your friendship means to me. You represent stability in my life. No matter in life the location or what direction we found ourselves, there was no direction that could cease our friendship. I appreciate your loyalty to me and not to what I had or could do for you. Thank you both for supporting my family in your own very special ways.

Elder Stan and *Deaconess Angelette Featherstone*: When my family had no home you took us in; when we were hungry, you fed us. Thank you for showing us your faith by the works you did (James 2:18).

Embrace Grace *investment hearers and readers*: Vincent C. Briscoe and Elisa Gilmore, thank you for investing your time to help me bring the books to its finality.

Table of Contents

Foreword

From a mother's heart, it gives me great joy and pleasure to have the blessing to be a part of my daughter Joy's life and ambitions. The Lord has blessed us to know Him as our personal Lord and Savior. Whatever we do in word or deed, we do it all for the glory of God. God wants to manifest Himself through our lives. The Lord has blessed my husband and I to see our children serve Him. Our youngest daughter Joy is serving the Lord with the heart of Jesus.

As a young woman, she has experienced the joys, hurts, disappointments, broken promises, and dreams upon her battle with her illness. All this while raising her children and being a submissive and wonderful wife to her husband as they work together in ministry. Through it all, she has learned to trust in Jesus with understanding; He has placed her on the wings of an eagle.

She has been broken to be blessed for the glory of God. The Lord is blessing her ministry, especially to women. Through God's supernatural power and compassion, He allows Joy to see things according to His perspectives, moving her with His wisdom and discernment to know God's will.

What a powerful and blessed woman of God she is! With a humbleness of heart, it is a privilege, blessing, and a source of great joy to foreword such a powerful book. As her mother, I have been pondering all these things in my heart. I'm excited about seeing the miracles of God working in her life. To God be the glory for the great things He has done and continues to do in Joy's life.

To all parents, let God be God in your child's life, and look for the miracles.

Love in Christ Jesus,
Joy's Mom, Minister Darlene Gallashaw

Introduction

I was told to get a walker and bedside commode and to expect my life to get worse, which caused my thoughts to be in conflict with each other. Though I initially was relieved doctors finally figured out what was wrong with me, my life later became filled with anxiety. I had to figure out how I could continue to fulfill what I was created to do after being diagnosed with multiple sclerosis in 2008.

In this book you will read about three events in my life that caused me great pain and suffering. You will see the impact it had on me and my family and how I overcame it. Victory in life was always something I greatly desired, but the process to obtaining it was not easy as I watched my dreams die. The ability to speak to someone who could help guide me through was not always available, especially in the midnight hours. There's nothing like the cries that are filled with the tears that come from the depth of your belly when you are unable to put words to the pain. Not being able to have the consistent companionship of someone who understands your mental, spiritual, and emotional pain only adds to the injury and isolation you feel. Yet the burden and desire to help others was still there, so was the longing to be in fellowship with others too! However, how was I supposed to help others understand that the pain and suffering I was experiencing was weakening my life-engaging senses? It was changing the way I interpreted life. My ability to respond to situations and others was altered because of the effect the pain and suffering was not only having on my life, but on my mind, body, and spirit.

Because I could not always call and reach someone due to the consistency of my pain, I turned to the Bible to see who suffered like me and what they did to overcome it. I found Paul and I had a lot in common. He prayed numerous times to ask God to heal him and take his pain away, as did I. When Paul prayed, he didn't get what he believed God could do; matter of fact, he didn't get a yes or no. He got another answer, which is what happened to me too. Paul's life intrigued me; how could he be a great ambassador and leader in the midst of his tremendous pain? I began following the steps that Paul took, which you will see below what those steps looked like in Paul's life. As you read this book, you will see what those steps looked like in my life through the challenging events I share. As I followed those steps, they led me to living a life overcoming daily and life altering challenges with the abilities to rise in leadership, travel, and fulfill my purpose.

This book was written with you in mind. Often times, I felt alone in my pain, abandoned by God, and frustrated with not being positioned better in life. I could not let another moment go by with the thought of not helping someone else with their pain and challenges. Together, you and I will face and overcome our challenges in life. Whether they are everyday challenges or life-altering situations, past or present, our dedication to the process of overcoming will position us for the brighter life and future we desire.

Here's the steps Paul took that empowered him to lead with authority in the midst of his pain and challenges:

- Paul *acknowledged* what he was going through—"a thorn in the flesh was given to me" (2 Corinthians 12:7b, NKJV).

- Paul *requested* his desire—"Concerning this thing I pleaded with the Lord three times that it might depart from me" (2 Corinthians 12:8, NKJV).

- Paul *accepted* God's response—"Therefore most gladly I will rather boast in my infirmities, that the power of Christ may rest upon me" (2 Corinthians 12:9b, NKJV).

- Paul *participated* and became a part of what God was doing in his life—"Therefore I take pleasure in infirmities, in reproaches, in needs, in persecutions, in distresses, for Christ's sake. For when I am weak, then I am strong" (2 Corinthians 12:10, NKJV).

EG

And He said to me, "My grace is sufficient for you, for My strength is made perfect in weakness."

—2 Corinthians 12:9a, NKJV

Section 1

THE GRACE
TO LIVE

Part 1

WHY DOESN'T GOD
JUST TAKE ME?

I must openly confess to you that when Maurette Brown Clark in 2007 came out with the song titled "It Ain't Over," I could not handle listening to that song. There is a verse in that song that says, "it ain't over until God says it's over." *I wanted God so badly to say it was over for my life!* I begged God to please just take me in my sleep! Trying to watch my children and husband become my caretakers when I was supposed to be taking care of them became unbearable.

Pain and suffering are real. It was difficult for me to acknowledge what I was going through, because I didn't want to feel or seem like I was defeated and that my situation won over me. Pain and suffering bring great challenges in our lives, interfering with us living effectively and operating at our full potential in our daily tasks, desires, and pursuits. As pain and suffering often do not seem to cease in our lives, how can we live at our fullest, completing all the things intended for us to accomplish? In the theme passage from the introduction, we will find the key steps to living out our full potential while accomplishing our lives' purposes in the midst of our greatest challenges!

In 2 Corinthians 12:7, I found the beginning of how to handle and overcome the pain in my life. Paul in this verse was in pain; he *acknowledged* it through saying, "a thorn in the flesh was given to me" (2 Cor. 12:7, NKJV). Even though Paul was preaching the gospel, spreading news all about his God who saves, he did not talk super spiritual as if he had no pain. He admitted that in the midst of God's goodness, he was disturbed by pain in his life. There comes a place in our lives where we must do like Paul and *admit/acknowledge* the truth of what we are really going through. In the last section of this book, we will discuss who you outwardly admit the truth to, but in this section it's important to first begin with admitting the truth to yourself. Much like Paul, we will never become overcomers if we don't *acknowledge* what we need to overcome. While we cannot stay in a pity party of what we are going through, we cannot falsify or ignore its existence.

I have seen and experienced generational curses reversed and stopped when someone was brave enough to admit what they were going through. Acknowledging the pain or problem brings us to our true reality. It is in our true reality we can see what is real vs. false; our awareness of it leads us to knowing how to face it and overcome it. My friend, well-known psychologist and author Dr. Celeste Owens, in her response to the familiar saying, "you cannot heal what you conceal," believes this to be true. She proceeds by expressing in order to heal, one must first acknowledge that there is a problem and, second, take the necessary steps to move forward. That moving forward process includes acknowledging and validating your feelings. Feelings can be misleading, but in the context of healing, they are not to be ignored. God gave us feelings for a reason and recognizing them is a key component to healing.

After a long ten-year journey of trying to discover what was happening to my health, in 2008 I was finally diagnosed with multiple sclerosis. It never ceases to amaze me how, once I *acknowledged* my fear of doing a spinal tap, also known as a lumbar puncture, the answer to what I was going through was found in the very thing I was afraid of. I heard so many horror stories of having it done, yet while I suffered, I refused to do it. Your words have the power to influence positively or negatively. When a person who has great influence in my life heard me admit to being afraid to do the procedure, the power of their words changed my defeated, doubtful perspective. Those words, and how they fueled while empowering my heart, will never be forgotten. They said to me that if their spouse could have the procedure done, I could too. Continuing to explain how women were built to endure pain, I was instructed to just look at the child birthing experience I had already been through. In that moment, reflecting back to me giving birth to my children made me clearly see how I not only endured the pain, I conquered it too! *Fear paralyzes you and keeps you from getting your true answer.* When I pushed towards what I feared and moved forward with the procedure, my long ten-year mystery came to an end! Doctors were able to see my spinal fluid was not normal, and, with confirming MRIs, they were able to finally, properly diagnose me.

The diagnosis of the incurable disease was not the reason I wanted my life to be over and why I couldn't handle listening to the song. When they diagnosed me, I was initially relieved they had finally figured out what was wrong with me after a long ten-year uncertainty with my health. However, the more faith I pushed myself to have the worst my health became, causing my hope, excitement, and joy to fulfill my role as a mother, wife and minister to diminish. My health got to the point of the doctor telling me to get a walker and a bedside commode. I was already struggling to feed myself and could not make meals for me or my family. I could not picture my husband and children having to take care of me like that for the rest of my life. I was only in my thirties, and besides, I was supposed to care of them, especially with the children being so young.

Paul *acknowledging* the pain he was experiencing was such a healthy thing for him to do. I read in Sean Grover's Psychology Today article "How to Recover When Life Crushes You: Life provides suffering, healing requires help" that "we have the impulse to rise and start moving again when life viciously knocks us down. But ignoring a serious injury will make it worse. Pain demands attention, it needs to be acknowledged and embraced before you can move on."[1] That article resonated with me. I understood if someone had broken a foot, they could not continue to function and flow through life effectively on that foot. They had to go to the doctor to receive instructions on how to heal properly and continue their day-to-day living. Paul did just that; he acknowledged something was causing him pain. He understood if he was going to continue in his day-to-day successfully, the pain in his life needed to be addressed.

I had to open up and be honest with God that I felt embarrassed. Here I was, a minister of the gospel lying in the bed, spiritually guiding and praying for people, as well as watching others get their breakthroughs. Yet, while my family and I were suffering, we together were watching our dreams die! My marriage was interrupted; the intimate communication between my husband and me was highly impacted. No longer did the two of us really talk about the daily decisions of our home, our finances, or just to hang out and swap stories about our days. Our sex life, marriage, and ministry dreams were seriously deceasing.

I missed out on those intimate conversations with my daughters and helping them transition from little girls into teens and young ladies. No longer could I be the number one fan in the bleachers at my oldest son's, Vincent Eric's basketball games. To watch his passion of playing the game diminish broke my heart! My children were somewhere around the ages of sixteen, twelve, ten, and six when they—except for the youngest—became my caretakers with their dad. When my oldest son was around fifteen or sixteen, he started working to pay for things his younger siblings wanted or needed.

It was even more embarrassing as so many thoughts consumed me, such as, *what happened to me? Was something wrong with me and my faith? What happened to my anointing? Did it leave?* There was a season where I prayed for sick people, and instantaneously, they were healed. I prayed for a woman who hadn't walked in years; instantly, she walked and now runs. I remember praying for one woman who lost her hair from cancer, and I received a report that the most beautiful hair grew back on her head. Why couldn't I speak to the mountains in my life and they be removed?

Part 2

DREAMS DIE
BUT GOD WON'T LET ME DIE

With my health deteriorating, along with each of my dreams, my family's dreams were rapidly deteriorating as well! On top of that, our house was being foreclosed on, which we will discuss more in the next chapter. This is when I kept praying, "if it ain't over till God says it's over, Lord please say it's over; Lord, let it be over. I don't want to be a burden, take me in my sleep." God wouldn't take me; He wouldn't let me die. *I wasn't created to die in that season, I was created to live.* God's Word says, "I have come that they may have life, and that they may have it more abundantly" (John 10:10b, NKJV).

How do you live an abundant life when everything about you and around you is deteriorating? As difficult as it was for me, I had to *accept* what God was allowing in my life and the life He was building for me. We can see in 2 Cor. 12:8-10 the second thing Paul did that kept him thriving in the midst of his pain:

> Concerning this thing I pleaded with the Lord three times that it might depart from me. 9 And He said to me, "My grace is sufficient for you, for My strength is made perfect in weakness." Therefore, most gladly I will rather boast in my infirmities that the power of Christ may rest upon me. 10 Therefore I take pleasure in infirmities, in reproaches, in needs, in per-

secutions, in distresses, for Christ's sake, for when I
am weak, then I am strong.

—2 Corinthians 12:8-10, NKJV

Paul *accepted* what God was doing in his life because he understood there was a greater picture of what God was doing. Accepting what God is doing is not to be confused with accepting the
sickness or whatever your thorn may be, nor that God won't heal
you from it. Many people think when it is said "accept what is
happening," that means they are accepting being defeated by the
problem. Absolutely not; don't accept the problem, as it will never change. Accept the promise that God said He was going to use
the problem to reveal Himself. The word "accept" is defined in
the Merriam-Webster Dictionary as to, "endure without protest
or reaction."[2] Paul, in our themed portion of scripture, did just
that. In 2 Cor. 9b, Paul does not react unwillingly to God after
God clearly answers him with not giving him what he desired. He
responds by *participating* in God's plan and accepting what God was
doing, "Therefore most gladly I will rather boast in my infirmities, that the power of Christ may rest upon me. Therefore, I take
pleasure in infirmities, in reproaches, in needs, in persecutions,
in distresses, for Christ's sake. For when I am weak, then I am
strong." God's plan is never for you to look bad, look weak, and
look like you've given into the problem, His plan is for others to
see beyond you and to see Him and His power.

Did you notice in the opening to the passage in 2 Corinthians 12:7, Paul starts with telling us there is purpose to his pain?
It reads, "a thorn in the flesh was given to me, a messenger of
Satan to buffet me, lest I be exalted above measure" (2 Corinthians 12:7, NKJV). There is more to you and me than what is
happening on the outside. There is an inner you that is easy to
go unnoticed and tends to get drowned out when you have to deal

with everything else outside of you. It is understandable how it is so easy to neglect the inner when we are simply trying to survive the situations. Paul was so much more than his affliction. Paul already had a testimony of his conversion from being someone who persecuted and killed the Christians to being one of God's leading men, who was spreading the gospel, converting others, and helping others grow in their Christian walk and faith.

In the midst of my suffering in bed for days and sometimes repeatedly for a month, there was more to me than what I was experiencing. Suffering with some sort of numbness, tingles, pain, disorientation and or weakness clouded my view. However, much like Paul after his conversion, there is a spiritual gift inside of each of us waiting with great expectation to be used and fulfilled. While I could not negate anything happening on the outside of me, I had to look at the invisible part of me, the part of us that God had seen first before we were born. God speaks in Jeremiah 1:5 (NKJV), and He says, "Before I formed you in the womb, I knew you; Before you were born, I sanctified you; I ordained you a prophet to the nations." God had seen something in the spirit about you and me, that our bodies are just the houses to hold all the purpose He had seen in the spirit. According to the previous verse, you and I have to take a look in the spirit realm and in our spirits to discover the purpose God saw for us before we were even born. In the spirit realm, God created the spirit of man to be full of life and purpose. While our outward man is deteriorating, our inward man is full of life and purpose waiting to be lived out. 2 Corinthians 4:16 (NKJV) says, "Therefore, we do not lose heart. Even though our outward man is perishing, yet the inward man is being renewed day by day."

That verse had become so applicable in my life. It was clear God wasn't going to take me, so I had a choice to either be the head or tail. I could be the head and, with God, take charge over my health, or I could be the tail and let my health and doctors run my life. It was not that I didn't do what the doctors recommended; with much research and understanding, I followed their advice. Research and understanding helped me to know which option they advised was best for me or to ask if they had another alternative if needed. It became clear the spiritual man (inward man) God formed in me had work to do. Whenever needed, I leaned on the doctor's best option that would put me in the best condition to accomplish the purpose God ordained inside of me.

Our inward man is where purpose is birthed; the renewing of the spirit is where our purpose matures. Do you know your purpose—the purpose that was created in you before your mother even found out she was pregnant with you? Do you know the spiritual gift that lies inside of you, waiting to be fulfilled through your God ordained, no-one-can-take-it-away purpose?

Part 3

THE FIGHT IS ON, BUT KNOW WHAT YOU'RE FIGHTING AND HOW TO FIGHT IT!

Fighting for My Health

My walking was deteriorating so fast in one season, my doctor at that time told me to get a walker. They told me to also get a bedside commode because I kept passing out from trying to walk to the bathroom. My mother's best friend gave me one of her walkers. However, when I asked my mother about the bedside commode, I remember her saying, "We're not going out like that." My mother, Minister Darlene Gallashaw, ministers to women, and right there, my mother was ministering and challenging me on *if this was the absolute best life I could live*, even in the midst of my pain and struggle. She was making me think what type of life I wanted to have, even though my life didn't look like it at the moment. Hearing the challenge and still knowing what the doctor wanted, my husband gently asked me what I wanted. I expressed to him my desire to be able to walk to the bathroom again. Every time I needed to go to the bathroom or, for that matter, anywhere around the house, my husband walked with me until I could do it on my own. When he wasn't there, my mother was with me.

You have to accept those who will walk with you through your journey. There are people who not only do not mind sacrificing their time, but they have been positioned to give you their time. I got frustrated at the "who wouldn't or didn't help me" until I realized who God assigns to help you, He gives the grace in the area He assigns them to help you in. If He assigned someone to financially bless you, then His grace was on their finances to give to you without their bank account hurting from their giving. They never lacked anything because they gave to you. God's grace was on one of my best friends, First Lady Terrie Stevenson, to drive four hours down from NY and bring two people who cleaned my whole house and did every ounce of laundry. His grace was on another best friend, Lady Kim Henderson, who prayed me through everything with great understanding because she was suffering too. God's grace shows up in so many ways! God's grace, which is known as His power and strength, was on my mother and husband to stand by my side and help me conquer that particular battle. God's grace was even upon my children as they helped me around the house.

The reason this section is referred to as "The Fight Is On" is because I had to fight through the reality of it being easier to just give up. It was easier for me to just lay in the bed and to roll over to use the bedside commode. Dealing with all the symptoms of MS and then, on top of things, not knowing where I was going to live after receiving the final foreclosure notice, was overwhelming. I was dreading my future. Fighting through the consuming thoughts of where my health would end up. All the while, continually thinking will the fight be worth it and will all of this even work? It really was easier to just give up. I couldn't imagine not working for something and not knowing how it would end and if I would even be okay or not. I had to spiritually fight through the feeling that *since God abandoned me, why shouldn't I abandon myself?*

This is where knowing what you're fighting is important. Even though God has promised us He will never leave us nor forsake us several times in His Word. I also had to realize *God never promised He was going to be a genie and give me what I want without me having to do some work to get it.* I began to fully understand our desires have to turn into action. Extensive research became my lifestyle every time the doctor told me how I was deteriorating and explained every symptom I was experiencing. I researched what I had to do to keep those things from affecting me drastically and I did them. No matter what I had to do between physical therapy and my diet, *I had to participate and position myself to receive my own miracle.* Not only do you and I have to pray that God will make us well, but there is also some work on our part. We can't just pray "heal me Jesus" and not be willing to put the food down that triggers the symptoms of the disease. Nor can we expect our bodies to become strong and maintain their strength without doing the work that is needed.

If I was going to have the life I desired, not only was I going to pray and ask God for a miracle, I would have to take part in what I was praying for. I would become responsible for the things I could.

I remember learning two types of miracles from my former pastor, also known as my spiritual doctor, Rev. Frederick C. Johnson. He is known as my spiritual doctor because when I first became ill, even with me being a member of another church, he fasted and prayed for me and wouldn't stop until God told him what I needed to specifically eat, drink, or supplement to take. I learned from him there are miracles where Jesus would just touch people, and they were instantly healed. Then there were miracles where people had to go do something, to be a part of their own healing like 2 Kings 5 where Naaman, the commander of a king's army, had leprosy. The Prophet Elisha told him to go dip in the dirtiest river, the Jordan; seven times after doing so, he was healed. So, it was time for me *"to go dip"* in my Jordan.

"To dip in my Jordan, to be a part of my own miracle" meant my lifestyle had to change significantly! The way I had to mother my children, be a wife to my husband, had to eat and exercise, all had to change! My diet changed significantly! Eighty percent of my diet was me saying no to the things I loved, and yes to the things I needed. Can we just say processed sugar is the devil?! It's so delicious, yet so addictive. If it was up to me, I would have eaten ice cream, cakes, and pies all day long. There was a season I was staying foggy. I had trouble processing, and it was difficult raising my foot to walk—it was the processed sugar! I learned this from fasting with the book *The 40 Day Surrender Fast*, which was facilitated and written by my friend, Dr. Celeste Owens. During that time, I gave up sweets, my mind became sharper than ever, and my foot barely drooped. Researching and eating a raw, fresh diet and consuming healthier choices was not foreign to me. I watched my father, Pastor Matthew Gallashaw, do it all the time, and I had to now follow the example that had been set before me. *You too will be an example of grace to all others watching, and much like Paul, your boldness and endurance through humility will win others over.*

I even changed my doctor. I had to find a doctor who was willing to allow me to participate in the wellness of my own health, not one who kept me dependent on them. The doctor I had would get so upset when I researched the side effects of medications and asked about alternatives. I found a doctor who believed in the patient taking as much charge over their health as they could. Matter of fact, my current doctor says, "use it or lose it" if you want to stay active, be mobile, and do the things that keep you mobile. My doctor believes lifestyle influences your health, and doctors are there to help you find the best option for your health and support you through your health journey. A huge thank you and shout out to Dr. Scott Newsome and PA Lisa Fox at John Hopkins Medicine. Thank you for being a vital part of my health journey!

Fighting for My Role in the House Again:
Once a Mom, Always a Mom!

Once my health became more stable where I could endure processing in depth conversations and my mobility increased, reengaging with my children was difficult. The years I spent having to miss out on a middle school graduation, volleyball, and basketball games were years that my kids felt neglected and empty. Matter of fact, one of my daughters at a workshop she was facilitating talked to some other young ladies about how she had to forgive me for not being there for her, even though she knew I had no control over what was happening to me.

When I first reengaged with my children, I came in like a strong force demanding their respect as their mom. However, because they felt abandoned by me, I had to earn my parental right and respect back. You might be thinking, "They should have had respect for you all along," and the reality to that statement is they didn't intentionally lose respect for me as their mom. When crisis hit, my voice and abilities as their mom were not able to be heard and felt, which left them having to go into survival mode and figure things out for themselves. When my voice was able to fully return, their position was "we already have it figured out." The natural progression of my voice of authority, love, and guidance from their birth to adolescence had been interrupted. Where my voice would have normally been heard through their transitional years, their voices, as well as their father's, was forced to become more of the guiding voice factor. This caused multiple arguments and head clashing, because while I was trying to reestablish my right to speak into their lives because I was Mom, they were fighting to defend and protect themselves from the pain of not having my voice and presence in their lives when they needed me the most.

I learned in order for them to regain their confidence and respect in me again, I had to allow them space where they could see me do the things I used to do and allow them to even witness how I learned to readjust myself to do those things again. Something so simple, as my kids would see me cooking again and think to themselves, "Oh wow, Mom can cook again, but this time she takes short breaks in between; there are even times she doesn't do anything afterwards because she's extremely tired from cooking." In their minds they were redeveloping their confidence in me again while thinking and understanding, *that's what her new normal now looks like.* Even when I began moving around more again, my children had to adjust to what that looked like. They had to go through a process of accepting me with a limp, a cane, and a need to hold on to someone for assistance. When I stopped demanding for my position to be back in their lives, I began to see their hearts and how they were trying to accept my frailty with the mother they once knew as "Wonder Woman."

The longing we have for a particular need in our lives can cause us pain. It pained me not to be emotionally present in my children's lives, as well as that I looked weak and not capable to them. That pain desired instant change and was causing me to demand they immediately see me differently. The more I demanded, the more they saw me as a controlling, arrogant person. I was pushing them away more. We have to make sure the pain from the longing of what we desire does not cause us to become arrogant in demanding things. That only leads to others putting up a protective wall in their hearts, as well as pushing them to avoid us and shut us out even further. It is important we discipline the direction in which the pain tries to lead our hearts. To fight for my motherhood, I had to win my children back by allowing them to fall in love with me all over again.

The progression to reengaging in this relationship began with me allowing them to observe and accept the new reality, and intimate interactions often developed around those things. Matter of fact many conversations were birthed from them asking me how I felt about not being able to do things the same way. My transparency with them opened them up and lowered their defenses towards me, and we began to feel more a part of each other's lives again! My answers did not always include what I knew God was going to do. I did not always respond with high faith answers; I simply told them how I felt. I expressed both joy and sadness times. Transparency and honesty grew their confidence in me as well as their respect for me. It made me a trusted advisor once again in their lives.

I'm Still Your Wife!

My husband and I were such a team. We talked about everything. Sitting under the leadership of our pastor, Pastor John K. Jenkins Sr., my husband was taught to honor me in our decisions and not make any major ones without us being in agreement. The only time my husband moved in a certain major direction without me onboard was if he felt strongly that he was hearing from God. I had learned from our First Lady, Trina Jenkins, the principle of how I had to operate delicately and wisely, because I never wanted to lose my honor by seeking to control my husband. These principles became such a challenge for us when I got back on my feet. Due to the declination of my health, my husband learned how to survive making decisions on his own pertaining to our family and things outside of it. To relearn how to merge our opinions and consider each other's feelings seemed impossible while trying to navigate through my desire for my husband's heart to safely trust me again.

It was difficult for us to merge as a team again. Our hearts were filled with our own individual survival mechanisms to protect ourselves so we could survive life's storms! My husband was inwardly filled with so much anxiety for my health, he was trying to wrap his mind around the thought of losing me. The thought of him losing me and me dying was one of the things that kept him from wanting to discuss everything with me as I began to get on my feet. He feared if he shared too much, I would relapse and go backwards. My heart was filled with so much doubt on if I could handle it, yet I was trying to prove to myself and him I could. I desired so bad for my husband's heart to safely trust me again.

In order for my husband and me to work as a team again in all areas of our marriage, we had to give each other a grace period. This was a time where, even though we knew each of us was aware of how to live in a wholesome marriage, how to communicate with the other, and how to consider the other's feelings, we didn't penalize each other for getting it wrong. In the midst of our painful arguments, we came to the realization we both were hurting. We both felt wounded and abandoned by God. Can you imagine that when you and your teammate are both wounded? How does the team play when all the players are injured? *We play through grace.* Grace doesn't always make things easier, and it doesn't mean you don't bring correction to things. Grace gives you the strength that can't be compared to anything else to peacefully endure the hard work of the process that gets you back on track. As God is so passionate about strong leadership, so is He equally passionate about strong unity.

JOY M. BRISCOE

Grace Questions

1. What do you need to *acknowledge* that you are going through? *(I admitted I was afraid of doing the spinal tap. I had to acknowledge it was hurtful for me to watch others get healed while I was getting worse. I acknowledged MS was causing me physical, spiritual, and mental pain.)*

_____

_____

_____

_____

_____

_____

_____

_____

_____

2. What are you *requesting* from God? *(I requested for God to heal me)*

_____

_____

_____

_____

_____

_____

_____

_____

_____

3a. What was God's response to your request?

_____

_____

_____

_____

_____

_____

_____

_____

_____

_____

3b. Have you *accepted* God's response to you? Why or Why not?

_____

_____

_____

_____

_____

_____

_____

_____

_____

_____

_____

3c. What will *accepting* God's response look like in your life? *(I never accepted the disease, as I would not be healed from it. I accepted it as a way for God to show His grace and how He chose to do it. Standing before people in my weakest moments is when He looks strong.)*

_____

_____

_____

_____

_____

_____

_____

_____

4. How will you *participate and be a part of* what God is doing in your life? *(I changed my doctor and my diet, exercised, and modified how I interacted with my children and husband.)*

_____

_____

_____

_____

_____

_____

_____

_____

> And He said to me, "My grace is sufficient for you,
> for My strength is perfect in weakness."
> —2 Cor.12:9, NKJV

Section 2

THE GRACE
TO LOVE

Part 1

LOVE IS A
COMPLICATED CHALLENGE

We all need love; we all want to be loved. According to Dr. Raj Raghunathan in Psychology Today, in our pursuit to be loved the need to love and care for others is just as strong of a desire.[3] The desire enhances our happiness levels. I have found in working with others and in my own life, giving and receiving love is one of the most challenging things. It can tend to be one of the most challenging because we all have different ways of receiving love, and most of the time, we give love the way we want it given to us. The challenge that is posed is how we give love may not necessarily be the way the other person receives it. That is why in so many households there's normally at least one child who grows up thinking their parents didn't love them the way they loved their siblings. The way they interpreted love was different than their siblings' interpretations, and their perception was according to their love language.

There was a season in my own life where I didn't feel loved by my husband. While he was lavishing me with expensive gifts and purchasing me a beautiful house and cars I loved, I still felt empty and that he didn't love me. The reason being was because he was loving me the way he received, understood, and perceived love, which was through receiving gifts. I just wanted him to simply vacuum a floor. The two ways I felt loved was through him doing things for me, also known as acts of service, and through him affirming me through words of affirmation.

It became extremely important for me to learn how to love myself before seeking love from my spouse. When you know how to love yourself you can teach others how to love you. The Bible is clear: it is irresponsible of us to love everyone else before we love ourselves. Mark 12:31 (NKJV) says, "You shall love your neighbor as yourself." This is telling us we must responsibly love ourselves first, before we give love to others. We responsibly know how to love our neighbors (others) the way we have first learned how to responsibly love ourselves. To love yourself responsibly is to understand what you need and how to tend to those needs. We are created mind, body, and spirit; if you don't know how to nourish all three you will not be able to effectively help nourish someone else's mind, body, and spirit. Your love language is a wiring of how you feel loved and appreciated. According to Gary Chapman's *The 5 Love Languages*, some feel appreciated when others spend time with them, others feel loved when they receive gifts, while those like me feel loved and appreciated when they receive words of affirmation or an act of service through their spouse and others doing things for them.[4] When I discovered how I was wired to be loved then shared it with my husband, he began loving me according to my love wiring needs. The question of why he didn't understand and know how to love me was removed. When we understand our own love wiring system, we become more in tune with someone else's and are better able to meet their needs.

Tending to your spiritual, emotional, and physical needs are a demonstration that you understand how to love yourself. When you know the discipline measures you need to put in your life, you will be able to teach others your boundaries and the lines that they cannot cross in your emotional, spiritual, and physical life. Knowing how to love yourself in entirety equips you with a greater understanding of how to pour love into those who are broken while teaching them how to love themselves too.

How do we love others when they can't give it back to us? This is the situation I found myself in; matter of fact, to harbor hatred, anger, and disappointment in my heart was easier and felt more fulfilling. At least, so I thought.

Simultaneously, when I was diagnosed with MS, the economy was crashing and my husband's job as a loan officer had become non-existent. People had a hard time grocery shopping, let alone buying houses. While I was lying in the hospital bed receiving an MS treatment, my husband received a call from his employer letting him know they were closing their doors. Right there, the cycle of our funds decreasing began; by that following year, the foreclosure notices had come, and we were evicted. We were praying and believing God would save our house and bring us through. God did bring us through but not the way we thought. *Have you ever believed God could do a certain thing, and He did not do it?* My husband really believed God would honor his heart to take care of his wife, and God would provide for all other needs as He did before. Wow, did we ever feel like God had abandoned us as we kept searching and wondering, "God where are you?" My husband applied for well over fifty-to-one hundred jobs, including ministry and pastoral opportunities with all of them closing in his face or no response at all. This was with the exception of my husband becoming a janitor at our church. We were so grateful for this; however, we were still faced with the responsibilities that exceeded the yearly income of that position, as well as the prior outpouring from the fifteen plus years my husband spent building his mortgage business. My husband, over time and with a clear conscience, said to me "Baby, let the house go, I choose to save and fight for you. The house can be replaced, you can't." With a look of both love and grief on our faces, we held each other close with knowing one day the sheriff would come to knock on the door and ask us to leave our dream home. After experiencing the impact of having to let our dream go, there is still today no regret, because one of our greatest losses had become one of our greatest love stories, as well as an affirmation of our love.

Part 2

THE LOVE
CHALLENGE INTENSIFIES

A certain family member we had to live with severely challenged my love! Matter of fact, I harbored anger in my heart because I could control them there, since I couldn't say anything to them. I wondered so much if they did not see the pain and embarrassment my family was already in. When the sheriff came to remove us from the home, it was an eventful day. A few days prior to them coming, I had just finished having a MS treatment due to having a relapse. That day was one of the most humiliating days for my family. When the sheriff asked us to leave, he and his workers, who came to put our things out, walked around the house looking for things they would take for themselves. They asked one of my daughters what her favorite treats in the pantry were, took them out, ate them all up, and laughed in her face. Our neighbors were providing drinks for my husband, children, and friends who tried to salvage whatever they could. Even with that niceness, still the embarrassing reality of us not being able to take care of our responsibility was present. Now the public was seeing what was hidden behind closed doors. The embarrassment of their possible thoughts of "where is their God whom they confess to serve" was there! As we navigated through that embarrassment, my husband grew to this understanding and lead us through our trying time, reminding us, "Remember, we serve God, God doesn't serve us."

How true that statement is. While it is important for us to pray and make our requests known to God, we have to remember He answers us according to His plan in life for us. The responsibility to work through God's plan felt like it was too much for me. I was already overwhelmed with the responsibility of taking ownership over my health. Now having this experience added to the responsibility of my personal growth. All the while, I was also trying to gain a greater understanding of what I was going through and how it pertained to my personal ministry. Watching God shape my children into who He wanted them to be was disheartening. To feel the impact as God was reconstructing my husband felt too great for me to bear! I was also consumed with feeling guilty for it being my fault we were losing it all, and had it not been for me, my husband could have gone out and fought through the economy to provide for us. I hope you can understand why I said in the previous section how I felt it was just easier on everyone if God took me, and that's why I kept praying, "Lord, please say it's over and take me now."

As I look back, I really hear the words of the song—"it ain't over 'til God says it's over"—and God saying, "It's not over Joy, it can't be over, I can't take you now. You going out like this is not a part of My plan." I really can tell you His plan is a powerful plan, and you and I have to work through the pain to set our eyes on the plan. Then we will be able to recognize the power that is working in us. Do you know how much strength and discipline it takes to not focus on the pain and work through it? That strength and discipline, that's God's power and grace working in and through us.

My most difficult person to live with needed all of God's power that worked in me. I understood I was going to be just one of the encounters and examples of God's power they were going to see and have. This individual had a temper that was easily offended, quick to boil, and could blow you out of the house while you were still standing in it. Their mentality was if you lived in their home, no matter your age, you belonged to them, they owned you, you governed your life according to their ways, and your time belonged to them. Whatever they wanted done and whenever they wanted it, you were expected to do it. This angered and grieved me so much. The conditions of the house in which we lived were not completely sanitized, which caused us great concern. As if that wasn't enough to see, my husband and children being treated in such an inhumane way was becoming unbearable. Because nothing could be said, I said a lot to that person in the secret places of my heart. By that point, I became extremely angry with God. I expressed to God my relationship with Him seemed like a love-abusive relationship; while I was loving Him, He was continually allowing me to go through so many things that by that point I felt used and abused by Him.

I was trying so desperately to understand why it wasn't enough that I was diagnosed with an incurable disease. That my family was laughed at, talked about, and ridiculed when we lost our home. Now, we were living with a person who enjoyed and felt good believing they were supposed to be sandpaper in the lives of those who lived in their house. All I can say is, I had to make a choice on if I was going to love God through all of this or go backwards in my health and life by harboring all the hatred and anger in my heart. At that turning point, I prayed God, "Please give me the grace to love." I didn't even know how to love someone who prided themselves on hurting others because they believed they were sandpaper, there to smooth others out.

One of the things that kept coming to my mind was, "In all your getting get understanding" (Proverbs 4:7b, NKJV). I kept trying to figure out what it was I wasn't getting with all this affliction I was going through. Then I heard, "Have you ever thought

they are afflicted too?" Then my eyes came off me and were fix-
ated on understanding them. They hurt others and took pride
in hurting others because they too were hurt. As a matter of fact,
they never graduated high school; they became the provider for
their siblings when they were in the seventh grade because their
father was an alcoholic. There was a huge turmoil in me—how
could I be moved with compassion for them while I secretly was so
angry, harboring hatred towards them and their behavior?

Here we were, living with someone who watched their child-
hood stop and their dreams die. All the while, they were probably filled with uncertainty for their future as they had to become
stability for their mother and siblings. I began to understand
what my family was going through probably brought back all the
insecurities and feelings they thought they left behind and tried
to escape every day. My prayer moved from, "Lord, give me the
grace to love" to me thanking the Lord for the grace He has already given me to love. I remember after one particular incident,
pulling my children into my room and letting them know I knew
they were hurting, and it was painful for me to watch. I further
expressed God gave us every tool we needed to use in every situation. When we say God's Word—the Bible—is our weapon, we look
to what's in the Bible for our situations and use it in our battles.
It was clear that Matthew 5:44 (NKJV) was the weapon for that
situation: "But I say to you, love your enemies, bless those who
curse you, do good to those who hate you, and pray for those who
spitefully use you and persecute you." God's weapons are not always easy to use but over time you will find as you use them, they
will provide comfort and empower you to push through the hurt,
pain, and anxiety of your situation.

Love is defined according to the Interlinear Bible on Bible-
StudyTools.com as to welcome, to entertain, to be fond of, to
love dearly.[5] This is the real love challenge: to love someone, to

be fond of them, to welcome them into our lives when they are mentally damaging and hurting us. There was so much conflict in me because I needed to protect my family from things and others that posed as ready to bring destruction in their lives. Yet here, I had to love and teach my children to love the one who seemed threatening to them. I had to let God's Word be above my reality while not ignoring our reality. I understood I had to seek help for my family's inner peace, aching spirits, and souls so our entire family went to therapy. This was all while helping and teaching my children to let their actions be love and to respect the position our loved one had in our lives. Simultaneously, we were financially building ourselves to seek a place of our own. Since the Word of God teaches us to wrestle not against flesh and blood, then I needed help going into the spirit realm to wrestle with the demons that had my family member bound. With that in mind, further support was requested and given by an intercessory prayer warrior for my family, as well as prayers for the one whom we lived with would be set free. There was a clear understanding of how their bondage was only seeking to hold us in bondage like they were. Captivity is a demonic mindset so while hurting people hurt people, captive people take other people as their captives.

Here was my opportunity to operate in my ministry gift to heal the brokenhearted, to loose the bonds of wickedness, to undo the heavy burdens, to help let the oppressed go free. When we say yes to walk in our ministry, we really don't know the dark places it will take us. At some point, we have to come to the place of understanding that *we are more secure and protected in walking in obedience in the dark places than to walk in disobedience outside of our purpose.* There I was, living in the broken circumstances of my own life while watching my family be broken by someone else. *Broken people break people.* Healing in the midst of that environment, which was filled with so much anger, oppression, and aggression, could only manifest itself through the tool we have now identified as love.

There was much navigation needed through deep hurts and anger, and sometimes God's silence. I remembered every time I got on an airplane, the safety instructions given by the stewardess would always alert us that, in the event of an emergency, we were to put our oxygen mask on first and then help others put theirs on. This also reminded me in the Bible where Jesus says, "You shall love your neighbor as yourself" (Matthew 22:39b, NKJV). Those were my instructions on how to use the "love tool." As mentioned before, I had to get help on how to love myself in the midst of all that was going on. My family got help so that they could feel loved and cared for. Once I began learning how to view my husband and me, along with how to build boundaries within our relationship to keep the external from affecting the internal, I was able to push past me to demonstrate concern and care to the one we all felt we were up against.

Demonstrating my love and care, as well as being fond of them, meant sometimes my husband and I found ourselves watching movies with them that they enjoyed. I recall one time they were telling me they weren't going to invite a close family member to an event they were having because of a falling out they had with them. This was the perfect opportunity not to beat them over the head with what the Bible says about fall outs. This was the perfect opportunity to help them see themselves according to God's Word.

Many times, we exhaust ourselves from telling someone to do the things God wants them to do and then become frustrated because they won't do it. When we understand we do not always naturally have intentions or desires to do what God's Word says, we begin to have a sensitivity to others and the opportunities to help plant God's way in their lives. Look for your opportunities to quietly apply God's Word in their lives so they themselves can be proud of their ownership of the concept and be compelled to operate by the principle.

As they proceeded to tell me why they weren't going to invite certain people, God's grace helped me to discipline myself to sit and just simply listen. Then I was able to graciously respond with first affirming I heard their hurt and frustration. After saying "I understand," I then responded gently with this question: "Do you think inviting them would show you are the bigger, more mature person?" That question showed my interest in them, their development, and how they would be perceived, while at the same time putting Philippians 3:12-14 in action in someone's life.

> Not that I have already attained, or am already perfected; but I press on, that I may lay hold of that for which Christ Jesus has also laid hold of me. Brethren, I do not count myself to have apprehended; but one thing I do, forgetting those things which are behind and reaching forward to those things which are ahead, I press toward the goal for the prize of the upward call of God in Christ Jesus.
> —Philippians 3:12-14, NKJV

God will use us in our most uncomfortable situations to implement His ways. There in that moment is the implantation of no longer pondering on what has angered you. Otherwise, it will interfere with you moving forward to obtain the reward that comes from the successful strides you have made.

Reconciliation is always God's plan. He demonstrated it when He sent His Son to die so that we would be reconciled back to Him. My husband and I, even after we were able to move and get a place of our own, always made sure the one who hurt and did us wrong knew we loved them. After some time, due to their health challenges, we spoke to them in person, and I repeatedly gave them kisses. My husband even told them it was an honor to serve them, and he looked forward to doing it. Those were our last words, actions, and final goodbyes—as the days followed, they passed away.

This section is dedicated to my father-in-law, Vincent Briscoe, who has now passed away. From the day I met you, you acknowledged me, loved me, and accepted and protected me as one of your own. Thank you for that. There are still days I feel I need you. You will forever be remembered, loved, and missed.

Your daughter-in-love,

Joy

Grace Questions

1. Who in your life do you need to *acknowledge* is challenging to love? Why?

_____

_____

_____

_____

_____

_____

2. What have you prayed and *requested* from God to see happen in your relationship with that person?

_____

_____

_____

_____

_____

_____

_____

_____

_____

3a. What has God spoken to you about that person and your relationship? *(God showed me their mental condition and all they had experienced that had made them the way they were.)*

_____

_____

_____

_____

_____

_____

_____

_____

_____

_____

3b. Have you *accepted* what God said? Why or Why not?

_____

_____

_____

_____

_____

_____

_____

_____

4. What do you need to do to *participate* and be a part of what God is doing in your relationship with that person?

_____

_____

_____

_____

_____

_____

_____

In all your getting, get understanding. His grace will empower and guide you through.

Self-Nourishment Page

Self-nourishment is vital in making sure you have the necessary fuel to stand up against the challenges in life!

Fill in how you nourish the following areas and how often. If you have not begun, please write down how you plan to and how you will make it a part of your day.

How do you nourish your:

MIND (this includes your emotions, feelings, mental health, and the ability to control your thought life):

_____

_____

_____

_____

_____

_____

_____

_____

BODY (physical activity, eating, etc.):

_____

_____

_____

_____

_____

_____

_____

SPIRIT (spirituality, your purpose, and what brings life to you):

_____

_____

_____

_____

_____

_____

_____

> Do you not know that you are the temple of God and
> that the Spirit of God dwells in you?
>
> —I Cor. 3:16, NKJV

Section 3

THE GRACE
TO FORGIVE

Part 1

CAN I JUST STAY ANGRY?

Aren't there some things we can remain angry about? Aren't we allowed to hold onto our anger and grudges towards someone for the things they have done that are so painful and unforgettable?

I kept havinge this reoccurring dream of my little two-year-old self and this boy having me pinned down. He's holding my arms down to make sure I don't move while he is having sex with me. Even though it was my little two-year-old self I kept seeing, that dream seemed so vivid to me. I later found out it wasn't just a dream; it actually happened to me! It's amazing how our brains are smart enough to lock something away. Later, we realize what has been locked away will manifest itself some way in our bodies because our bodies are smart enough to understand something toxic doesn't belong there, and it needs to rid itself of it!

There was a period in my marriage I struggled greatly to be intimate with my husband. Before we were married, I didn't struggle at all to be touched by him; however, when we got married, I couldn't handle being touched by him. True intimacy had to take place in my life, as my husband calls it "intomeyousee" (In-to-Me-You-See). It was time for me to take a personal look into my inner self to see what was happening in my intimate life. Why had it become so backwards? Why was right (being touched in my marriage) wrong to me and wrong (being touched while not married) right to me? An article in Time explained the effects that both sexual and emotional abuse has on women. It explains that when a woman has been sexually abused at a young age, visual changes on the brain were seen on imaging to the somatosensory cortex, which is the area that processes input from the body to create sensation and perceptions.[6] Our perception of being touched is not fully developed when sexual abuse has taken place at a small age. Our brain's growth development has been damaged and interrupted. In summarizing the article from Time, depending on the amount and severity of the abuse, you would more easily perceive pain instead of touch in certain areas.[7]

I had no idea how to heal from such abuse nor how to fully recover my brain development and emotions. The only thing I knew to do at that time was to ask God to help me heal. I was putting up so much distance between my husband and me. I understood that distance was not laying a foundation for a healthy, long lasting, fulfilled marriage. Healing is a process requiring multiple steps. It was crucial I healed from this pain, because not only did it happen to me when I was two years old, but again when I was five; the sexual abuse happened multiple times as well.

Telling a trusted confidant was shockingly the beginning to my healing. When someone affirms you, there is this empowerment that comes over you to move in truth and no longer in darkness. Many survivors of sexual abuse suffer through the thought that no one will believe them. Many survivors have been ignored and rejected. Their growth has been stunted because the only negative affirmation that has taken place is the misuse of their bodies. When someone affirms you, they are providing healthy approval in your life. I began to notice the healthy approval in my life was the beginning of my brain unlocking the secrets it held onto for so long. Holding on to those secrets of sexual abuse was causing me to replay it over and over again. Like other survivors, the low self-esteem, shame, and guilt that came from these abuses were hid with the secret and was rehearsed over and over in my mind as well.

JOY M. BRISCOE

The Bible tells us, "Therefore if the Son makes you free, you shall be free indeed" (John 8:36, NKJV). The more I told my testimony of what happened and how God healed me, the more empowered I became as one of God's leading ladies. The first step of *acknowledging* what I had gone through and receiving the *affirmation* was the beginning of being set free. Timing is everything! Who you share the events with is just as important. We will talk more about who you should share traumatic events with in the next section.

Even though I tried my best to hide this secret, I felt like I was going to bust at the seams if I had to keep holding it in. It is so important for us to understand that while there are temperaments (personalities) that are naturally explosive, many times a person will explode from the underlying cause of the pain that is looking for an opportunity to come out. Many times, pain pushes the temperament to its extreme. Those who are natural introverts and suspicious of others become more secluded and lack confidence in themselves and others. Others who seek happiness and a life of enjoyment push the pain down deeper. They escape to their own idea of enjoyment in life. They would rather live in the idea of life's enjoyment instead of the reality of what caused their pain. Those who seek peace and are laid back, often times are found not wanting to do the work that is required to push through and heal from the pain.

Part 2

WHEN AND WHO
DO I SHARE WITH?

How do you know when it's time to share? *Look for the open door.* Sharing with my confidant was prompted during a time right after hearing a speaker at a workshop talk about her own sexual abuse. It led us to talking about the speaker's testimony, and then the door was open for me to share my own experience. In that moment, my confession of what happened to me led to the next step of my healing, which was through my confidant's acceptance of me. The fear of rejection that lurks in one who has been sexually abused is broken though acceptance. One of our greatest fears is rejection because we feel like damaged goods, and *who would accept me?*

We must not fall into the desire to share our story in the form of a testimony when healing has not taken place. Here the Word of God tell us, "And they overcame him by the blood of the Lamb and by the word of their testimony" (Revelations 12:11, NKJV). What is key here is the word "testimony." A testimony is defined by Merriam-Webster as "a public profession of religious experience."[8] Our testimony is to tell what happened and our *experience* of what God did. It is beneficial for us and our listeners to tell our testimony after God, according to what His plan has accomplished in us and the things He wants to accomplish through what He has allowed. Other than that, if we speak in the name of "we are telling a testimony," we may find ourselves speaking from a place where we are telling what happened to vent, getting it off our chest, and, many times, looking for empathy and acceptance.

Who Do You Share With?

If you noticed, I shared with my closest, trusted confidants first. Those who you share with must be trusted confidants in your life. It is never their responsibility to go tell anyone this information for you. Being sexually abused leaves such pain and insecurity in you; the last thing you need is for it to be shared at a time that leaves you feeling vulnerable again. Often times, God uses your confidants as a source of relief, relieving your heart and head-space while you sort through your healing process.

Sexual abuse and traumatic events are giants with so many layers. One layer is facing the reality of what really happened, then facing the giant of inner reconciliation of what took place. One of my layers was understanding who I really believed needed to know before I continued to reveal the testimony of this heal-ing. That's when my parents entered my healing process and, in essence, brought closure to it. This took place when I was mature and strong enough to face the giant of having an adult conversa-tion about being sexually abused. My brain had developed a matu-rity and understanding of the traumatic event and its full impact on me, along with the inner peace and reconciliation. This was the true sign I was ready to have a mature conversation about it. I was extremely fortunate to have parents who accepted my truth of the event. They prayed, supported me, and sought how they could help me recover from that event.

Many are not as fortunate to have that. This is why you must conquer the healing of other layers of your giant first, before en-tering into discussions and possibly being questioned about it. Often times, when the abused is being questioned about what happened, they tend to feel defensive and that the questions are signs of others doubting them. While that may be the case in some instances, being healed provides you with an inner peace to not fight against them but to speak your piece and be at peace with their doubt. This helps you to leave the conversation reconciled while feeling a sense of resolution. Even though their unacceptance will hurt, it usually doesn't sting as bad because you have already found healthy acceptors in your counselor and confidants, along with your inner peace and reconciliation. You mentally have to be at a place where others hurting you doesn't injure unresolved pain. It will only escalate your pain and dig a deeper wound, resulting in lashing out and trying to prove what happened. There's a mature confidence that covers you when you are healed with inner reconciliation and peace.

My initial thought was I would keep this secret until the abusers passed away, and then I would tell. There was even a time when I felt bold enough to talk with one of the abusers before even thinking of writing a book about it. I was in counseling and mentioned that thought, and the counselor had me play out the scenario. The counselor played the abuser and had me act out how I was going to approach them. They calmly portrayed the denial the abuser could potentially say and how they recalled the event differently—as it being my way of showing I loved them and/ or I wanted it. The reality hit that the abuser's admittance to the sexual abuse may never come and their denial or recollection of the event would hurt me more, delay my healing, and produce more anger and pain in me.

Often times, many who have been abused believe it helps them to confront the abuser. In my experience not only with my situation but with working with others, those who are hurting need affirmation from the one who hurt them, as well as that they acknowledge the pain they have caused. The acknowledgement brings assurance to the one who is hurting, helping them to believe the one who has done the hurt understands the damage they have done. When that acknowledgement does not happen, the emotional process to move forward and heal is often held up, leaving one seeking how to compensate their emotional deficiency. Telling a confidant, counselor, and spiritual guide became a safe place for me, and I believe you will find it safe too. You will find with them the ability to receive the key things needed for your guidance to healthy healing and affirmation, acknowledgement, and acceptance.

Part 3

CAN MY SPOUSE HELP ME HEAL?

Absolutely! The best way my husband helped me heal was to become my greatest friend and confidant. Friendships hold this endearment of concern while not feeling the responsibility to fix each other. The marriage relationship often becomes so boggled down with the need to always make everything right. The responsibilities of marriage can tend to outweigh the concerned yet free ability to simply just be present and available without trying to fix each other.

I have found it to be true that the one with the problem is the one who usually holds the solution in their hands, not just in my own life but in the lives of others I have had the opportunity to counsel and guide. They just need the space and time to discover it and process through it. One of the greatest things my husband gave me was his patience to allow me to discover and go through the process to heal. For him to demonstrate his understanding of my pain and to discipline himself not to comment consistently on the impact my healing process was having on him and our marital interactions was much needed. When a spouse forces their needs on you, it takes away the other spouse's free will to respond. The other spouse will be reminded of how their free will was taken from them during their trauma, which can cause their healing to be disrupted and damaged again.

The spouse's unconditional understanding and support aides greatly in the healing process. However, the spouse who needs healing benefits from receiving help from a professional or someone equipped to handle and guide others through their pain. In a marriage, because the supporting spouse is already, through much love, carrying great responsibilities on their shoulders, it becomes difficult for them to help guide their hurting spouse through the pain without trying to fix them. While a spouse watches their mate navigate through life altering situations, it can be the most difficult thing for them to watch and bear. Their need to urgently see their hurting spouse fixed will damage and interrupt the healing. The question the onlooking spouse must ask while desperately desiring the full fulfillment of the marriage is, "Do I want a healthy, whole marriage that will last a lifetime, or do I want just a temporary gratification?" When needed, it is extremely beneficial for the supporting spouse to attend counseling sessions with the other spouse to aid them in learning how to support and maintain their marriage while the process of healing is taking place. It also provides the supporting spouse a space where they can be fueled through receiving support themselves.

Part 4

WHAT DOES BEING
HEALED LOOK LIKE?

God's healing touch and His wisdom go hand and hand. You really can't have one without the other. God's wisdom doesn't let you forget the incident; God's wisdom matures you and helps you grow from His perspective on the incident.

During my healing process, I became so angry with God. I stopped going to church, and I didn't want to have anything to do with Him. I cried out in anger to Him, "How could You let this happen to me? Not only when I was two, but then at the age of five, after I knelt in my apartment at the sofa with my Mom and I gave my life to You. Shortly after that, You allowed me to be sexually abused multiple times. I don't understand You! How in the world could You do this to me!?" God's response shocked me! He said, "I'm glad you're speaking to Me again, I'm big enough and able to handle your anger with Me. I'm angry too!" I was sitting on my bedroom floor leaning up against my bed in utter amazement at what God said; I quickly responded, "Huh?" My heart instantly reconnected with God, as I could not believe I just heard God Himself say He felt like how I felt and was angry with them too.

God told me He saw what they were going to do before they did it. Because He gave man a free will to make their own decisions, when He saw the decision they made to abuse me, it angered Him so much that He knew through their sinful actions they would condemn themselves to hell. In His anger, He decided to give them a decision to choose Him and ask Him to forgive them or leave their ultimate fates in their hands. That's when I realized God and I had more in common than I thought! We both were enormously angry. The only difference was His anger was more with their decision and mine was more with the person.

God is passionate about the decisions we make. He has already made a way for us to be able to make the best decisions for our lives that will also compliment other people's lives as well. He has already released such an enormous amount of love and grace that is waiting for you and me. We just have to decide to receive it. God's love in our lives reminds us of why we live, and God's grace powers us through the godly life we live. What's amazing is He gave His grace and love when He saw me at my absolute worse, before I even knew how to look pretty with putting my make up on, look and act like a godly lady, and choose nothing but to serve Him. He saw me when I was doing everything wrong, and yet He gave me His best. He sent His son Jesus to die for you and me. He knew the wrongs we would do that would lead our lives to a life of condemnation. It was only going to be through the choice of me asking God to forgive me and receiving His Son Jesus that would set me free.

Part of the guilt I felt that was weighing me down so much was from my understanding of how I was forgiven so many times for my wrong doings. So, how could I remain in so much anger and not give others what had been given to me? This was a difficult part in my process of healing because what was done to me seemed so wicked and unforgiveable.

There are certain people who holding on to pain is more comfortable for them. I was one of them. I found comfort in my pain because, for me, it represented how I would have rather remembered and hated you than to be free of my pain thinking I had let you off the hook. Nor did I know how to let go of the pain that pierced me from the sexual abuse; it had become a part of my normal regimen to dress it up and carry it along with me.

I kept hearing others say, "Forgive and forget." That made no sense to me. I could not just dismiss what they did to me, nor could I forget about it. The more I accepted God sent His Son Jesus to die not just for me but for those who did me wrong and abused me, the more strength I had to accept what God allowed to happen to me. The more I accepted it, the more my eyes were open to see those who abused me were seriously lost and needed to find God for themselves. Why was I, through my anger, holding onto their dirty issues? The same way I had to work my issues out with God, they too needed to work out their dirty issues with Him on what they did to me. I had to let what they did go; if not I was paying the price that they needed to pay for themselves. My health was suffering more from holding that anger in; however, my anger was deceiving me. It had me believing my abusers were being punished from my anger and, through my anger God, would see the extent of how He hurt me. The freedom and full restoration I needed from the abuses happened when I let go of the anger. I let go of my anger towards them because I realized my anger was not making them stand before God and be accountable for their own actions.

Forgiveness doesn't let the other person off the hook; it frees you from the anger, frustration, and all spiritual, emotional, and physical reactions that are attached to it. Forgiveness means I give my rights up to punish the one who did me wrong. Forgiveness doesn't mean for you to forget what happened. Forgiveness allows you to walk in freedom with the ability to wisely assess situations.

I spent a season raising my girls from such an angry, anxious, fearful place. I was desiring for my girls to not experience what I went through, so instead of guiding them, I yelled at them from fear about how they dressed and their behavior that could cause someone to abuse them. Had I been free from my pain, I would have been able to wisely assess things which would have afforded me the opportunity to simply, lovingly guide them about the dangers that are out there. Forgiveness allows you to wisely discern who has good intentions towards you and your family and who you should not leave your children in the care of. I have watched and worked with leadership from pastors on down, who lead from such an angry, hurt, and insecure place that, unintentionally, those following them become hurt. Letting go and forgiving frees you to interact and lead from such a gracious place of life in and out of the home.

The best representation of healing is when you live your fullness in purpose and not in pain. Paul says in Philippians 3:13b-14 (NKJV), "but one thing I do, forgetting those things which are behind and reaching forward to those things which are ahead. I press toward the goal for the prize of the upward call of God in Christ Jesus." There is a goal that far exceeds the pain. One of my daughters asked me how I was strong enough to have four children and was shocked that I would've had more had it not been for my health. She said childbirth is a lot of pain, and yet I did it four times. I told her it was extremely painful, but after I had each child, the enormous amount of love and joy that filled my heart for them made the vividness of the pain diminish and caused me not to dwell on it. I was so consumed with loving them that I didn't look back, nor did I any longer need to care and tend to that pain. I was more concerned with seizing the moment by tending to them. I was so consumed with them being there and raising them to be healthy contributors to society. In childbirth, when the pain comes, you have to tend to the pain because the pain means something is happening, the baby is moving downward, and your body is preparing itself for what's about to come. Had I tried to keep the baby in and not deliver it, the pain would have never ended, resulting in trauma to my body. If you are still in pain, have bitter and/or excessive anger, and feelings of the memory of what someone has done to you, that is a good indicator that you have not resolved the issue in your life. Holding on to the pain is like trying to hold the baby in, resulting in more devastation and trauma to your body and life.

That's what Paul was teaching—it's not that you don't remember what happened. I can discuss each of my childbirth experiences. However, the intense pain I felt then is not vivid and present now. When pain has our attention and focus, we are not able to fully set our eyes on what is in front of us to move us forward. We are then stuck in one place, even though we look like we are in motion. Did you notice Paul said, "I press," while some versions say, "I reach," meaning moving forward doesn't always come easy. You have to get a determined mind that you will push past what has caused you pain. Pushing past is to never be confused with not dealing with the pain; you will only be able to pursue what lies beyond the pain if you have healed and reconciled it. Your inner peace is crucial for you to remain focused on obtaining the prize you were destined to have! Your prize could be a healthy marriage, other relationships, and/or operating in your gift and calling! I encourage you to do an assessment and search yourself to see where you are on a scale from one-to-ten, with one being the lowest level. Are you troubled by the pain and still seeking resolution from it? What number are you? Again, where are you on the scale from one-to-ten with being able to peacefully move forward to obtain your prize and goal without being distracted, consumed, or triggered by the pain or memory of it?

Grace Questions?

1. What and/or who do you need to *acknowledge* has hurt you?

_____

_____

_____

_____

_____

_____

_____

_____

_____

2. Are you able to forgive them? If no, why not?

_____

_____

_____

_____

_____

_____

_____

_____

_____

_____

3. What does forgiveness look like in your life?

_____

_____

_____

_____

_____

_____

_____

_____

_____

4. What do you need to *accept* from God as it pertains to what happened to you? *(I had to accept that God gave man free will, and just like Jesus died for me, God sent His son Jesus to die for those who hurt me too.)*

_____

_____

_____

_____

_____

_____

_____

_____

_____

_____

_____

5. What do you need to do to heal from the pain? *(I went to counseling and forgave.)*

_____

_____

_____

_____

_____

_____

6. What are you moving forward to be able to do? What is your goal? *(Paul didn't get stuck in his pain; he moved forward because he had a goal to reach and a prize to obtain.)*

_____

_____

_____

_____

_____

_____

**God has a special plan for you! Nothing has happened to you that will not fit in and be used in His plan for your life! There's a special plan design page for you on the next page.

God has a plan and purpose for everyone's life. Pray and ask God what yours is if you don't already know it. Please write your plan and purpose for your life, then your goals on how to achieve it.

Plan and Purpose

_____

_____

_____

_____

_____

_____

_____

Goals

_____

_____

_____

_____

_____

_____

_____

"For I know the plans I have for you," declares the
LORD, "plans to prosper you and not to harm you,
plans to give you hope and a future."
—Jeremiah 29:11, NIV

Conclusion

Even in the midst of the most challenging storms, we can look forward to fulfilling our purpose. Life does not always turn out the way we desire. We will experience both highs and lows during our lifetime. Becoming a person who knows how to live, love, and forgive in the most challenging circumstances empowers you to live your utmost life, fulfilling all that you were created to do!

In order to live at the highest quality of life, total healing of your mind and spirit is required! It was never intended for us to flow with toxicity living on the inside. Toxins eat at you and destroy you. It will only be through understanding and implementing the necessary life changes you need to make that will bring you to your full awareness of yourself, strength, and needs. Many times, we walk around looking for what we believe we need, when often, it is the toxin looking to be fed. It is when we get to the true root of what has caused the toxins in our lives that we are able to free ourselves of them. This allows our bodies to flow in more of its truer and natural state.

Determining your lifestyle change may initially be thought of as limitations in your life. Often times, those very limits help us set up the necessary, healthy boundaries in our lives. No longer are there limitations of what we cannot do, but rather boundaries helping us to define what cannot be crossed.

Because we often hear about living a "limitless" life, we often believe God has rejected us through our interpretation of our life altering circumstances as limits God has put on us. The Word of

God in Psalm 119:71 (NKJV) says, "It is good for me that I have been afflicted, That I may learn Your statutes." It is in our afflictions that we learn God never intended for us to live without limits and how to flourish in them. From the beginning of time, when He created Adam and Eve, He told them their limits, which were not to eat the fruit from a certain tree. God's protection for us is found in the limits He places on us. When Adam and Eve went outside their limits, they stepped outside of God's protection and brought death upon us all. To reject what God is doing in your life is to reject the grace, strength, power, and protection He has already provided and wants to give to you!

When we no longer live a life rejecting the way God is trying to remake us into His new creations through our circumstances, it is in those moments we learn how to properly flow, as well as nourish ourselves and others. When your mind is in a rejective state it causes you to miss out on flowing in the full creativity and understanding needed so you can thrive in the midst of your challenges!

Having your mind and spirit reconciled with life and God is where you will find the most creative ways to do all the things needed to overcome your challenges! It's time to release your thoughts and ways of doing things and *embrace* what God is doing in your life!

Get ready for a life filled with wisdom, power, strength, and creativity to overcome obstacles when you choose to **Embrace Grace!**

JOY M. BRISCOE

About the Author

Joy M. Briscoe was born in Philadelphia, PA and primarily raised in Willingboro, NJ. She is the CEO of JoyNspiresU Inspiration Co., where she inspires others to face and overcome their challenges of life while providing *H.OP.E.* She is helping them to *heal* from their past, *overcome* their present obstacles, *position* them for a brighter future, and *equip* them with empowering tools to sustain and thrive in life. Please visit joynspiresu.com for more information.

She has been married for twenty-eight years to her college love, Rev. Vincent C. Briscoe. The key to her becoming one with her spouse in their marriage was her love for God, as well as becoming her husband's best friend, trusted advisor, and teammate. Joy's understanding of the great influence the wife has in her marriage while remaining submitted to her husband has led her to working with wives. She has designed a special program to empower and develop the wife in her influential role while providing hope to her. Joy also speaks for Sunday morning services, at marriage events, conferences, retreats, and special events both individually as well as alongside her husband. From their union, they have four children ranging from the ages of eighteen to twenty-eight.

After the whirlwind of the diagnosis of MS hit her home and she watched her twelve-year-old take on her motherly duties, she developed a *Ladies in Leadership Training* specifically geared for wives and moms. This training empowers the wife and mother, beginning with aiding her in properly understanding herself and who she was created to be in addition to the influence and impact she has on the home. This training brings enlightenment on how she will either help or hinder those in as well as out of the home with the attributes God has given her.

Joy is no stranger to the church. She grew up in a household where her father pastored and where both parents ministered to the community and served in the church. After rededicating her life to the Lord and walking with consistent faithfulness to God, in 2002 she became a licensed minister at the First Baptist Church of Glenarden, where Pastor John K. Jenkins Sr. is the Senior Pastor.

For over twenty years, Joy has helped church leaders, pastors, and their churches in various ways. She has aided in their individual developments, as well as the development of those under their care in understanding and fulfilling their purposes in serving the church. Joy also serves as the spiritual advisor for Women of the Word Ministry in Philadelphia, PA.

Joy's opportunity to be exposed to various church leaders allowed her to see leadership operate in its finest, as well as leaders who led through their hurts while serving. Through watching these experiences, she developed a deep passion to aide in the growth and development in the leaders' healing of their minds, bodies, and spirits.

Get inspired to live your best life even in the midst of great challenges! Connect with Joy on:

• FACEBOOK @Joy M. Briscoe

• INSTAGRAM @joymbriscoe

• TWITTER @JoyMBriscoe

• EMAIL @hope@joynspiresu.com

Endnote

[1] Sean Groover, "How to Recover When Life Crushes You: Life provides suffering, healing requires help," Psychology Today, Sussex Publishers, June 16, 2017 https://www.psychologytoday.com/intl/blog/when-kids-call-the-shots/201706/how-recover-when-life-crushes-you?amp#Publishers, LLC.

[2] "Accept", Merriam -Webster.com Dictionary, January 11, 2021 https://www.merriam-webster.com/dictionary/accept.

[3] Raj Raghunathan, "The Need to Love," Psychology Today, Sussex Publishers LLC, January 8, 2014, https://www.psychologytoday.com/us/blog/sapient-nature/201401/the-need-love.

[4] Gary Chapman, *The Five Love Languages* (Chicago: Northfield Publishing 1992, 1995).

[5] "Agapao," Bible Study Tools, Thayer and Smith. The KJV New Testament Greek Lexicon https://www.biblestudytools.com/lexicons/greek/kjv/agapao.html.

[6] Maia Szalavitz, "Sexual and Emotional Abuse Scar the Brain in Specific Ways," Time, June 5, 2013, https://healthland.time.com/2013/06/05/sexual-and-emotional-abuse-scar-the-brain-in-specific-ways/.

[7] Szalavitz, "Sexual and Emotional Abuse Scar the Brain in Specific Ways."

[8] "Testimony", Merriam-Webster Dictionary, January 8, 2021, https://www.merriam-webster.com/dictionary/testimony.